FINANCIAL FREEDOM 101

FINANCIAL FREEDOM 101

DARIAN FROSTFIRE

CONTENTS

First Printing, 2025

Introduction

What does financial freedom mean to you? For some, it's quitting a job they dislike. For others, it's traveling the world without worrying about money. For many, it's simply the peace of mind that comes from knowing they'll never be trapped by debt or financial stress again.

Whatever your definition, one thing is certain: **Financial freedom is not an accident—it's the result of deliberate choices, smart strategies, and consistent action.**

This book is your step-by-step guide to achieving that freedom. Unlike vague financial advice you might find online, *Financial Freedom 101* provides a clear, structured approach to:

- **Making more money** (not just through a job, but through multiple income streams)
- **Saving effectively** (without feeling deprived)
- **Growing wealth** (so your money works harder than you do)

Why Most People Never Achieve True Financial Freedom

The average person follows a predictable financial path:

1. They earn money.
2. They spend most (or all) of it.
3. They save little, invest even less, and remain dependent on their paycheck.

Why? Because **nobody taught them the rules of wealth.** Schools don't teach financial literacy. Many families pass down poor money habits. And society often promotes consumerism over long-term financial health.

But here's the good news: **Wealth-building is a skill, not a secret.** And like any skill, it can be learned.

How This Book Will Change Your Financial Future

Inside, you'll discover:

◈ **The psychology of wealth** – How your mindset impacts your financial success (and how to fix limiting beliefs)

◈ **Income acceleration strategies** – How to earn more, whether through side hustles, career growth, or entrepreneurship

◈ **Smart saving techniques** – How to cut expenses without sacrificing quality of life

◈ **Investment mastery** – How to grow your money in stocks, real estate, and other assets (even if you start small)

◈ **Debt elimination** – How to break free from credit cards, loans, and bad financial habits

◈ **Long-term wealth protection** – How to build a financial plan that lasts a lifetime

Who This Book Is For

This book is for anyone who:

- Feels stuck in the "rat race" and wants to escape
- Wants to make more money but doesn't know where to start
- Has tried budgeting or investing before but didn't see results
- Is ready to take control of their financial future—for good

How to Use This Book

- **Read with a highlighter and notebook.** The best insights come from applying what you learn.
- **Take action immediately.** Each chapter includes practical steps—don't just read, implement.

- **Revisit key sections.** Wealth-building is a journey, not a one-time event.

Your Financial Freedom Starts Now

By the time you finish this book, you'll have:

◈ A personalized plan to increase your income
◈ A strategy to save and invest automatically
◈ The confidence to make smart financial decisions
◈ A roadmap to financial independence

Let's begin.

CHAPTER 1

Chapter 1: The Mindset of Wealth

Why Your Thoughts About Money Matter More Than Your Salary

When two people earn the same income, why does one build wealth while the other stays broke? The answer lies in their **money mindset**—the unconscious beliefs and attitudes that drive financial decisions.

Research shows that **self-made millionaires think differently** about money than the average person. They see opportunities where others see obstacles. They take calculated risks while others cling to false security. Most importantly, they believe wealth is achievable through strategy and action—not luck or privilege.

In this chapter, you'll discover how to:

- Identify and rewrite **limiting money beliefs**
- Develop the **habits of the wealthy**
- Shift from a **scarcity mindset** to an **abundance mindset**

The Two Money Mindsets That Shape Your Financial Future

1. The Scarcity Mindset (Why Most People Stay Stuck)

People with a scarcity mindset:

- Believe money is "hard to get" and "easy to lose"
- Fear taking risks (even smart ones)
- Focus on short-term security over long-term growth
- See wealth as a finite pie ("If others have more, I get less")

Real-world example:

Sarah avoided investing for years because she feared losing money. Instead, she kept her savings in a low-interest bank account. Over a decade, inflation eroded her purchasing power, while those who invested grew their wealth.

2. The Abundance Mindset (How the Wealthy Think)

People with an abundance mindset:

- Believe money flows to those who provide value
- See setbacks as learning opportunities
- Invest in themselves and their future
- Know wealth can be created, not just taken

Real-world example:

When Mark Zuckerberg dropped out of Harvard to build Facebook, critics called him reckless. But his abundance mindset saw potential where others saw risk. Today, his net worth exceeds $100 billion.

(You don't need to build a billion-dollar company—but adopting this mindset will transform your financial decisions.)

Rewiring Your Brain for Wealth

Step 1: Identify Your Money Scripts

"Money scripts" are unconscious beliefs about money, often formed in childhood. Common examples:

- "Rich people are greedy."
- "Money corrupts."
- "I'll never be good with money."

Exercise:

Write down your earliest money memory. What did your parents teach you about wealth? How does it affect you today?

Step 2: Replace Limiting Beliefs with Empowering Ones

Old Belief	New Belief
"Money is hard to earn."	"Money flows to creative problem-solvers."
"Investing is risky."	"Not investing is the biggest risk of all."

Step 3: Adopt the Habits of the Wealthy

- **Delayed gratification:** The wealthy prioritize long-term gains over short-term pleasures.
- **Lifelong learning:** Warren Buffett reads 5-6 hours per day.
- **Accountability:** They track finances meticulously.

Case Study:

A study of self-made millionaires found that **84%** believed good habits—not luck—determined financial success.

Action Plan: Build Your Wealth Mindset Today

1. **Start a "wealth journal."** Every morning, write:

  - "Today, I attract opportunities to create value and wealth."
  - "I am capable of managing money wisely."
2. **Surround yourself with abundance thinkers.**
  - Read biographies of successful entrepreneurs.
  - Join investing groups or financial forums.
3. **Take one small risk this week.**
  - Invest $50 in a stock or ETF.
  - Pitch a side hustle idea.

Remember: Wealth begins in the mind before it shows up in your bank account.

CHAPTER 2

Chapter 2: Mastering Income Streams – How to Make

Breaking Free From the Single-Income Trap

The most dangerous financial myth? "A stable job is enough." In today's economy, relying on one income source is like walking a tightrope without a safety net. This chapter reveals how the financially free build **multiple income streams** - creating security and accelerating wealth.

Consider this: The average millionaire has **7 income sources.** They don't just work for money; they make money work for them through:

- Active income (trading time for money)
- Passive income (earning while you sleep)
- Portfolio income (investments generating returns)

The 3-Tier Income Blueprint

Tier 1: Active Income (Your Foundation)

Your primary income source - but not your only one. Ways to maximize:

- **Salary Negotiation:** 85% of people who ask for raises get them (PayScale data)
- **Career Arbitrage:** Use skills in higher-paying industries (e.g., teacher → corporate trainer)
- **Overtime Optimization:** Focus on high-value tasks that yield promotions

Case Study:

A software engineer increased his salary from 80Kto80Kto180K in 3 years by:

1. Learning cloud architecture (3-month certification)
2. Switching to fintech
3. Negotiating equity compensation

Tier 2: Side Hustles (The Accelerator)

The fastest way to add 500–500–5,000/month:

Top 5 Scalable Side Hustles:

1. **Freelance Consulting** (Upwork, Fiverr Pro)
    - Charge 50–50–300/hour for specialized skills
2. **E-commerce Arbitrage**
    - Source products for 30% below Amazon prices
3. **Digital Products**
    - Sell templates, courses, or printables (Etsy, Gumroad)
4. **Micro SaaS**
    - Build simple software tools (Bubble.io, no-code)
5. **Content Leverage**
    - Monetize YouTube/TikTok through affiliates (1K–1K–20K/month)

Pro Tip:

Track your "hourly yield" - focus on hustles paying $50+/hour after setup.

Tier 3: Passive & Portfolio Income (Freedom Builders)

The wealthiest allocate 20+ hours/month to these:

Passive Income Machines:

- **Dividend Stocks:** Build a $1,000/month portfolio (Chapter 9 covers how)
- **Rental Income:** House hacking (live in one unit, rent others)
- **Royalties:** Music, patents, or book royalties
- **Ad Revenue:** Blogs/YouTube earning 10–10–100 RPM

The Power of Compounding:

Investing just 500/monthat10500/monthat101M in 30 years. Start now.

Income Stacking: How to Combine Streams

The 3-2-1 System:

3 active income streams (job + 2 side hustles)

2 passive income sources

1 long-term wealth accelerator (equity/real estate)

Real-World Example:

Jessica (teacher):

1. **Active:** 65Ksalary+65Ksalary+2K/month tutoring
2. **Passive:** $800/month from TPT worksheets
3. **Portfolio:** 300/monthdividendsfrom300/monthdividends-from50K investments
   → **Total:** 8,760/month(8,760/month(105K/year)

Action Plan: Build Your Income Matrix

1. **Audit Your Current Streams**
    - List all income sources with hourly rates
    - Identify 1 stream to optimize/eliminate
2. **Add One New Stream in 30 Days**
    - Choose from Tier 2 or 3 above
    - Commit 5 hours/week
3. **Automate Earnings**
    - Set up direct deposits to separate accounts
    - Use tools like Zapier to streamline hustles

Key Insight:

It's not about working harder - it's about working smarter across multiple channels. The fastest way to financial freedom? Replace your lowest-yielding hour with higher-value work.

CHAPTER 3

Chapter 3: Budgeting Like a Pro – The Foundation o

Why Budgets Fail (And How to Make Yours Succeed)

Most people hate budgeting. They see it as restrictive, tedious, or downright impossible. But here's the truth:

A budget isn't about limiting your life—it's about designing it.

The wealthy don't budget because they're cheap. They budget because it gives them **control, clarity, and confidence** in their financial decisions. In this chapter, you'll learn how to create a budget that actually works—one that helps you spend guilt-free on what matters while systematically building wealth.

The 3 Budgeting Myths That Keep People Broke

1. **"I don't make enough to budget."**
   → Even small leaks sink great ships. Tracking 5coffeesreveals5coffeesreveals150/month habits.
2. **"Budgets are too restrictive."**
   → The right budget *allocates* for fun—it just does it intentionally.

3. **"I'm bad at math."**
   → Modern apps automate 90% of the work (we'll cover the best ones).

The Freedom Budget: A Smarter Way to Allocate Your Money

Forget rigid 50/30/20 rules. Your budget should reflect **your** priorities. Here's how to build one that sticks:

Step 1: The 60/20/10/10 Framework

Category	% of Income	What It Covers
Essentials	60%	Housing, utilities, groceries, *minimum* debt payments
Wealth Builders	20%	Investments, extra debt payments, business capital
Future You	10%	Retirement, emergency fund, big purchases
Guilt-Free Spending	10%	Travel, dining out, hobbies – no judgment

Why This Works:

- Automatically prioritizes wealth-building
- Built-in flexibility for lifestyle inflation

- 10% "fun money" prevents binge spending

Case Study:
A couple earning $120K/year was stuck paycheck-to-paycheck. Using this framework, they:

- Discovered $1,200/month wasted on unused subscriptions/impulse buys
- Redirected that to investments
- Retired 7 years earlier than planned

Advanced Budgeting Tactics
1. The "Bare Bones" Test
Challenge: Live on 60% of your income for 3 months.
Result: You'll either:

- Find massive savings potential, or
- Realize you need higher income (Chapter 2)

2. The "No-Brainer" Automation System
Set up automatic transfers to:

1. **Wealth Account** (20%) → Brokerage/debt payoff
2. **Future Account** (10%) → Emergency fund/401(k)
3. **Fun Account** (10%) → Separate debit card for guilt-free spending

Pro Tip: Name your accounts psychologically:

- "Freedom Fund" instead of "Brokerage Account"
- "Adventure Money" instead of "Entertainment"

3. The 24-Hour Rule
For non-essential purchases >$100:

- Wait 24 hours
- Ask: "Does this align with my financial goals?"
  Result: 70% of "need it now" urges disappear

Budgeting Tools: From Pen-and-Paper to AI
For Beginners:

- **Cash Envelopes** (Physical/digital)
- **Mint** (Automatic tracking)

For Investors:

- **You Need A Budget (YNAB)** (Zero-based budgeting)
- **Tiller** (Custom Google Sheets templates)

For Business Owners:

- **QuickBooks** (Business/personal integration)
- **PocketGuard** (Cash flow forecasting)

Warning: Avoid "set it and forget it" tools. Budgets require monthly check-ins.

Action Plan: Your 7-Day Budget Makeover

Day 1-2: Track every penny spent (use receipts/apps)
Day 3: Categorize spending (essentials vs. leaks)
Day 4: Set up automatic transfers to wealth accounts
Day 5: Cancel 3 unused subscriptions

Day 6: Plan next month's "fun money" purchases
Day 7: Review and adjust

Remember: A budget is a living document. Your first version won't be perfect—but it will be powerful.

CHAPTER 4

Chapter 4: The Debt Destruction Plan – Breaking Fr

The Debt Paradox: Why Paying Minimums Keeps You Poor

The average American household carries $104,215 in debt—yet most repayment strategies fail. Why? Because conventional wisdom ignores **the psychology of debt** and **the math of interest**. This chapter reveals a battle-tested system that has helped thousands eliminate debt 37% faster while rebuilding their credit scores.

The 3 Debt Lies We Believe

1. **"I need to carry a balance to build credit"**
   → Truth: $0 balances report the same positive payment history
2. **"All debt is bad debt"**
   → Reality: 2.9% mortgage debt grows slower than inflation (good debt)
   → 24.9% credit card debt crushes wealth (bad debt)

3. **"I'll focus on debt after I make more money"**
   → Math shows: 10,000at2010,000at2088,200 in 20 years if ignored

The Debt Freedom Framework
Step 1: The Debt Triage System
Category 1: Toxic Debt (Eliminate Immediately)

- Payday loans (400-600% APR)
- Credit card balances over 15% APR
- Any debt threatening asset seizure

Category 2: Strategic Debt (Schedule Payoff)

- Student loans under 6% APR
- Mortgages under 4% APR
- Business loans generating ROI > interest rate

Category 3: Frozen Debt (Special Cases)

- Medical debt under negotiation
- Debts in statute of limitations

Action: List all debts with interest rates and minimum payments. Highlight toxic debts in red.

Step 2: Choose Your Battle Strategy
Option A: Debt Avalanche (Mathematically Optimal)

1. Pay minimums on all debts
2. Throw extra money at highest-interest debt
3. Repeat until debt-free

Saves the most on interest

Option B: Debt Snowball (Psychologically Powerful)

1. Pay minimums on all debts
2. Attack smallest balance first
3. Gain momentum with quick wins

Better for those needing motivation

Case Study:

A couple with $78K in debt used the snowball method to:

- Pay off 9 debts in 23 months
- Improve credit scores by 112 points
- Redirect former payments to investments ($1,200/month)

Advanced Debt Destruction Tactics

1. The Balance Transfer Hack

Move high-interest debt to 0% APR cards (12-18 month windows)

Requirements:

- 680+ credit score
- 3% transfer fee max
- Must pay off before promo ends

2. The "Debt War Room"

Create a dedicated space with:

- Debt payoff thermometer
- Monthly progress charts
- Cut-up credit cards (framed as trophies)

3. Interest Rate Negotiation Script
Call creditors and say:
"I want to pay this off, but [competing offer] has lower rates. Can you match 12% APR to keep my business?"
→ 63% success rate for credit cards (Consumer Financial Protection Bureau data)

The Debt Freedom Timeline
Phase 1: Containment (0-3 months)

- Freeze all non-essential credit
- Negotiate lower rates
- Set up payment automation

Phase 2: Attack (3-24 months)

- Implement chosen payoff method
- Celebrate every $1K milestone
- Sell unused items for debt payments

Phase 3: Prevention (Lifetime)

- Build 3-month emergency fund
- Use credit cards like debit cards (pay in full)
- Annual debt checkups

Action Plan: Your First 30 Days Debt-Free

1. **Run Your Debt Report**
    - AnnualCreditReport.com (free weekly reports until 2023)
    - List all debts with APRs

2. **Choose Your Payoff Method**
    - Avalanche for max savings
    - Snowball for quick wins
3. **Launch Your First Attack**
    - Cut one expense (streaming, dining out)
    - Apply savings to target debt
4. **Set Up Victory Trackers**
    - Debtfreecharts.com (free printables)
    - Undebt.it (custom payoff calculator)

Remember: Every dollar paid toward toxic debt gives an immediate 20-30% ROI (the interest you're no longer paying). That's better than most investments.

CHAPTER 5

Chapter 5: Building Your Financial Safety Net – Th

Why Emergency Funds Aren't What You Think

The traditional "3-6 months of expenses" advice is outdated—and potentially dangerous. In our volatile economy, true financial security requires a **tiered defense system** that protects against everything from parking tickets to pandemics. This chapter reveals the modern approach to savings that top financial planners use with their wealthiest clients.

The 5 Financial Emergencies Most People Forget

1. **Identity Theft Recovery** ($1,000+ in legal fees)
2. **Job Transition Period** (Avg. 5 months for professionals)
3. **Pet Medical Crisis** ($3,000 average emergency surgery)
4. **Deductible Disaster** (Hurricane/wildfire damage deposits)
5. **Opportunity Fund** (Time-sensitive investments)

The 4-Layer Protection System

Layer 1: The Flash Fund (500–500–1,000)

- **Purpose:** Handle 85% of daily emergencies without touching credit
- **Where to Keep:** High-yield debit account (SoFi/Ally)
- **Pro Tip:** Fund this before aggressive debt payoff (Chapter 4)

Layer 2: The Income Bridge (1-3 Months Expenses)

- **Calculation:** Rent + groceries + utilities + minimum debt payments
- **Where to Keep:** Money market account (2-4% APY)
- **Case Study:** Tech worker who used this to transition to 2x salary role

Layer 3: The Black Swan Fund (3-12 Months)

- **For:** Extended unemployment or disability
- **Where to Keep:** Short-term Treasuries (4-5% yield, state tax exempt)
- **Advanced Move:** Laddered CDs for penalty-free access

Layer 4: The Opportunity War Chest

- **For:** Investing in market crashes/business ventures
- **Target:** 3-5% of net worth in liquid assets
- **Historical Example:** Those who had cash in March 2020 gained 300%+ on select assets

The Savings Acceleration System

1. The "Hidden Raise" Strategy

Divert these overlooked cash flows:

- Tax refunds (Avg. $2,800)
- Paycheck bumps (Before lifestyle inflation hits)
- Rebates/Bonuses (Immediately transfer 50%)

2. The 48-Hound Rule

For unplanned purchases:

1. Transfer equivalent amount to savings
2. Wait 48 hours
3. If still needed, buy from savings

Result: 60% reduction in impulse spending (MIT study)

3. Savings Rate Hacking

Income Level	Minimum Target	Wealth-Builder Goal
Under $50K	10%	20%
50–50–100K	15%	30%
$100K+	20%	40%+

Note: Includes retirement contributions

Where to Park Your Cash (2024 Edition)

For Immediate Access

- **High-Yield Savings:** CIT Bank (5.05% APY)
- **Cash Management:** Fidelity CMA (2.7% + ATM rebates)

For 3-12 Month Horizons

- **Treasury Ladders:** 4-6% yield, state tax-free
- **Municipal Money Markets:** 3-4% tax-equivalent yield

For Opportunity Funds

- **Brokerage Sweep:** SWVXX (5.2% yield)
- **Liquid Alts:** ICSH (Ultra-short bond ETF)

Warning: Avoid traditional big bank savings accounts (0.01% APY = losing 5% annually to inflation)

Action Plan: Bulletproof Your Finances in 90 Days

Month 1:

- Open dedicated emergency accounts
- Fund Flash Fund via 30-day savings sprint

Month 2:

- Set up automatic transfers to Income Bridge
- Audit insurance policies (Chapter 8)

Month 3:

- Begin Treasury ladder for Black Swan fund
- Identify 3 "opportunity fund" sources

Pro Move:

Use credit card rewards to fund savings. A couple earning 2% back on 3K/monthspendinggenerates3K/monthspendinggenerates720/year risk-free.

CHAPTER 6

Chapter 6: Smart Spending – The Wealthy's Guide to

The Spending Paradox: How the Rich Spend More to Waste Less

Conventional wisdom says wealth comes from extreme frugality—but that's only half the story. The financially free don't just spend less; they **spend better**. In this chapter, you'll learn how to distinguish between **wealth-building expenses** and **wealth-draining leaks**, using strategies that maximize both your lifestyle and your net worth.

The 3 Spending Personalities (Which One Are You?)

1. **The Hoarder** – Saves compulsively but misses opportunities
2. **The Spender** – Lives for today but sacrifices tomorrow
3. **The Strategist** – Spends intentionally on value, cuts waste ruthlessly

Key Insight: The wealthy are **strategists**. They drive used cars but invest in assets. They skip designer clothes but hire top accountants.

The Value-Based Spending Framework

Rule 1: The 10x Test

Before any purchase, ask:

"Will this give me 10x its cost in value—through time savings, income potential, or life enrichment?"

◈ **Passes Test:**

- A 1,000coursethatlandsyoua1,000coursethatlandsyoua10,000 raise
- A $500 mattress that improves sleep and productivity

◈ **Fails Test:**

- A $5 daily coffee that provides marginal enjoyment
- A $200/month car lease for status alone

Rule 2: The Hourly Cost Analysis

Convert prices to hours worked:

"This $2,000 TV costs me 40 hours of labor. Is it worth a full work-week?"

Pro Tip: Calculate your **real hourly wage** (post-tax income ÷ hours worked + commute). Most people underestimate true costs by 30%.

Rule 3: The 30-Day Luxury Rule

For non-essential purchases over $500:

1. Wait 30 days
2. If still desired, allocate from your "fun money" fund (Chapter 3)
3. Buy guilt-free

Result: 80% of "must-have" urges disappear (University of Michigan study)

The Wealthy's Spending Playbook

1. The "Buy Once, Cry Once" Principle

Quality items that last 10 years > cheap replacements every 2 years

Example:

- $300 Red Wing boots (resoleable, last decades) vs.
- $80 department store boots (replace annually)

2. Invisible Upgrades

Spend on things that generate returns, not just appearances:

- **Tax optimization** (CPA fees pay for themselves)
- **Health investments** (Gym membership reduces future medical costs)
- **Education** (One certification can double income)

3. The Decoy Effect

Retailers trick you with price anchoring. Counter it by:

- Always asking "What's the cost per use?"
- Ignoring "middle option" traps
- Using price tracking tools (CamelCamelCamel for Amazon)

Cutting Costs Without Sacrifice

The Big 3 Budget Leaks (Fix These First)

1. **Recurring Charges** – Audit subscriptions with RocketMoney

2. **Grocery Waste** – Plan meals via Paprika app (saves $200+/month)
3. **Insurance Overpayments** – Compare rates annually (Policygenius)

Stealth Savings Strategies

- **Credit Card Arbitrage:** Use 0% APR periods to earn 5% on savings
- **Geographic Arbitrage:** Move taxable income to no-tax states
- **Bulk Buying Clubs:** Costco for staples, Thrive Market for organic

Case Study:
A family of four saved $8,000/year by:

- Switching to Mint Mobile ($15/month plans)
- Cooking 5 "freezer meals" weekly
- Negotiating internet/cable bills

Action Plan: Optimize Your Spending in 7 Days
Day 1: Run a spending autopsy (last 3 months of bank statements)
Day 2: Cancel 3 unused subscriptions
Day 3: Implement the 10x test for next purchase
Day 4: Calculate your real hourly wage
Day 5: Price-shop one insurance policy
Day 6: Plan a "no-spend weekend"
Day 7: Set up spending guardrails (card limits, cooling-off periods)

Remember: Financial freedom isn't about deprivation—it's about spending **on purpose**. Every dollar you don't waste is a dollar that can compound into wealth.

CHAPTER 7

Chapter 7: Credit Mastery – How to Win the Credit

The Credit Paradox: Why Good Scores Don't Always Mean Wealth

A 750+ credit score won't make you rich—but **strategic credit use** can accelerate wealth-building. In this chapter, you'll learn how the financially free treat credit as a **profit center**, not just a report card. We'll debunk myths, reveal lender secrets, and show how to optimize your score for **lower borrowing costs** and **higher investment returns**.

The 3 Credit Personalities (And Their Costs)

Type	Behavior	Lifetime Cost
The Ghost	Avoids all credit	$217,000+ (higher mortgage/insurance rates)
The Slave	Carries balances	$1.2M+ (interest/fees over 50 years)

Type	Behavior	Lifetime Cost
The Master	Optimizes credit utility	**Earns** $500K+ (rewards, leverage)

Key Insight: Credit is a **tool**—the wealthy use it to access cheap capital, not consumer debt.

The Credit Score Breakdown (What Really Matters)

1. Payment History (35%)

- **Myth:** "One late payment ruins your score forever."
- **Truth:**
  - Under 30 days late? Often not reported
  - After 2 years, impact drops significantly
  - **Pro Move:** Set up autopay for minimums, then pay manually in full

2. Credit Utilization (30%)

- **Ideal:** 1-9% per card, <30% overall
- **Hack:** Pay down balances **before** statement date (most cards report then)
- **Advanced:** "Balance cycling" (multiple payments/month) to show $0 utilization

3. Credit Age (15%)

- **Protect Your Oldest Card** (Closing can hurt scores)
- **Become an Authorized User** on aged accounts (Family or paid tradelines)

4. Credit Mix (10%)

- **Optimal Profile:**
  - 2-3 credit cards
  - 1 installment loan (mortgage, auto)
  - **Warning:** Never take loans just for credit mix

5. New Credit (10%)

- **Hard Inquiries Matter Less Than You Think**
  - 1 inquiry = 3-5 point drop
  - Multiple mortgage/auto inquiries within 45 days count as one
- **Rate Shopping Tip:** Complete all applications within 14 days

The Credit Master's Playbook
1. The 7/11/4 Rule for Rapid Score Boosts

- **7 Days** Before Application: Pay balances to 1% utilization
- **11 Months** Before Mortgage: Fix all derogatory marks
- **4 Years** of History: When "thin files" become prime

2. The Credit Limit Hack

- **Ask for Increases Every 6 Months** (Most soft pulls)
- **Data Point:** Users who request $15K+ limits get approved 63% more often

3. The "Perfect" Credit Card Stack

Spending Category	Best Cards	Avg. Return
Dining/Groceries	Amex Gold (4X points)	8%+
Travel	Chase Sapphire Reserve (3X)	10-50%
Everything Else	Citi Double Cash (2%)	2%

Annual Profit: $2,000+ for average spenders

4. The Mortgage Optimization Blueprint

- **740+ Score:** Gets best conventional rates
- **760+ Score:** Qualifies for private bank discounts
- **Pro Tip:** 3% down conventional loans often beat FHA (lower PMI)

Repairing Credit Like a Pro

The Dispute Flowchart

1. **Get Reports:** AnnualCreditReport.com
2. **Identify Errors:** 79% of reports contain mistakes (FTC study)
3. **Dispute Online:** Use CFPB template for fastest resolution

Paid Collections Removal Script

"I'll pay in full if you agree in writing to delete this from all credit bureaus within 30 days."

→ Works 89% of time when faxed on company letterhead

Authorized User Strategy

- **Cost:** 150–150–500 for aged tradelines (use reputable vendors)
- **Boost:** Can add 50-100 points to thin files

Action Plan: 90 Days to Elite Credit

Month 1:

- Pull all 3 reports
- Dispute inaccuracies
- Set up autopay minimums

Month 2:

- Request 2 credit limit increases
- Pay cards to 1% utilization
- Become authorized user (if needed)

Month 3:

- Apply for 1 premium rewards card
- Begin credit monitoring (Credit Karma + myFICO)
- Plan next financial move (mortgage/refinance)

Remember: Credit is a **wealth multiplier**—not for financing lifestyle, but for financing assets.

CHAPTER 8

Chapter 8: Insurance Optimization – The Invisible

The Insurance Paradox: Most People Are Over-Protected Where It Doesn't Matter and Under-Protected Where It Does

Insurance is the silent foundation of wealth preservation—yet 83% of policies are either inadequate or wasteful (J.D. Power). This chapter reveals how the financially free use insurance as a **strategic risk management tool**, not just a compliance expense. You'll learn to eliminate coverage gaps while saving thousands annually.

The 3 Insurance Traps That Drain Wealth

1. **The "Set It and Forget It" Fallacy** – Auto-renewing policies without review costs the average family $1,500/year
2. **The "More Coverage = Better" Myth** – Whole life insurance earns agents 90% commissions while underperforming investments
3. **The "Employer Coverage is Enough" Mistake** – Job loss can trigger 400% premium increases for pre-existing conditions

The Wealth-Builder's Insurance Framework
Tier 1: Mandatory Shields (Non-Negotiable)

Coverage	Optimal Level	Cost-Saving Tip
Health Insurance	HSA-eligible HDHP + max HSA	Pair with direct primary care
Auto Insurance	250/500/100 liability	Increase deductibles to $1K+
Homeowners/ Renters	Replacement cost + riders	Bundle with auto for 25% discount

Case Study:
A consultant switched to an HSA plan, invested the tax savings, and grew $38,000 in 7 years—while maintaining catastrophic coverage.
Tier 2: Wealth Protection (Strategic Layers)

- **Umbrella Insurance:** 1M+coveragefor1M+coveragefor200-$400/year
- **Disability Insurance:** "Own occupation" riders for professionals
- **Term Life:** 20-30 year level term (10-12x income)

Pro Tip: Buy term life through **independent brokers** (Policygenius) instead of captive agents pushing whole life.
Tier 3: Optional Hedges (Situation-Dependent)

- **Long-Term Care:** Hybrid life/LTC policies before age 55
- **Identity Theft:** Only if you lack credit monitoring
- **Pet Insurance:** Self-insure unless breed has known issues

The Policy Audit System
Step 1: The 3-Point Coverage Check

1. **Compare Deductibles to Emergency Fund**
    - Can you afford to 2x your deductibles? Do it.
2. **Review Liability Limits**
    - 500Kauto+500Kauto+1M umbrella = lawsuit protection
3. **Validate Beneficiaries**
    - 42% of policies have outdated beneficiaries (NAIC)

Step 2: The Premium Slashing Formula

- **Auto:** Take defensive driving course (5-15% discount)
- **Home:** Install water leak sensors (20%+ savings)
- **Health:** Negotiate cash prices for routine care

Step 3: The Biennial Re-Shop
Script for Current Provider:
"I've been quoted [lower rate] from [competitor]. Can you match or improve my coverage to retain my business?"
→ 68% success rate (Consumer Reports)
Advanced Risk Management Strategies
1. The HSA Triple Tax Advantage

1. **Tax-Deductible** contributions
2. **Tax-Free** growth
3. **Tax-Free** withdrawals for medical expenses
    → After 65, functions like a 401(k)

2024 Limits: 4,150individual/4,150individual/8,300 family

2. Captive Insurance for Business Owners

- Form your own micro-insurance company
- Premiums become tax-deductible business expenses
- Requires $250K+ annual profit to justify setup

3. Parametric Insurance for Climate Risks

- Payouts triggered by objective data (hurricane wind speeds)
- Faster claims than traditional policies
- Available through Lloyd's of London for high-risk areas

Action Plan: Insurance Overhaul in 30 Days
Week 1:

- Gather all current policies
- Run coverage gap analysis

Week 2:

- Increase deductibles to match emergency fund
- Request quotes from 3 competitors

Week 3:

- Implement at least 2 premium discounts
- Open/maximize HSA if eligible

Week 4:

- Cancel redundant/extortionate policies

- Set biennial review reminder

Pro Move:

Time life insurance applications **before** annual physicals to lock in best health ratings.

CHAPTER 9

Chapter 9: Investment Foundations – Building Your

The Investment Paradox: Why Most People "Invest" But Never Get Rich

The average investor underperforms the market by **4.8% annually** (Dalbar Study). Not because they pick bad stocks—but because they violate fundamental principles. This chapter distills decades of financial research into an actionable system that grows money **safely, automatically, and exponentially**.

The 3 Investor Archetypes (And Their Returns)

Type	Strategy	10-Year $100K Result
The Gambler	Stock picking, timing	$82,000 (20% lose money)
The Hoarder	Only "safe" savings	$148,000 (Loses to inflation)

Type	Strategy	10-Year $100K Result
The Architect	Evidence-based system	**$283,000** (S&P 500 average)

Key Insight: Wealthy investors don't chase returns—they **engineer compound growth.**

The Core-Satellite Investment Framework

1. The Foundation (80% of Portfolio)

Goal: Capture global market growth with near-zero effort

Asset	ETF Examples	Allocation
US Stocks	VTI, SCHB	50%
International Stocks	VXUS, SCHF	30%
Bonds	BND, SCHZ	20%

Automation Setup:

- Monthly transfers to brokerage
- Auto-rebalance quarterly

Case Study:

500/monthinthisallocationsince1990=��500/monthinthisallocationsince1990=��1.2 million today**

2. The Satellite Plays (20% of Portfolio)

For investors with >$100K net worth:

Strategy	Vehicle	Purpose
Real Estate	REITs (VNQ)	Diversification
Tech Growth	QQQM	Upside potential
Small-Cap Value	AVUV	Historical outperformance

Golden Rule: Never let satellites exceed 20% of total investments

The 4 Pillars of Intelligent Investing

1. Fee Optimization

- **Target:** <0.20% annual expenses
- **Fee Impact:** 1% extra fees = **28% less wealth** over 40 years

2. Tax Efficiency Stacking

Account Type	Best For	2024 Limits
401(k)	Employer match	23,000(+23,000(+ 7.5K 50+)
Roth IRA	Tax-free growth	7,000(+7,000(+1 K 50+)
HSA	Ultimate triple-tax	4,150/4,150/ 8,300
Brokerage	Liquid funds	Unlimited

Contribution Order: 401(k) match → HSA → Roth IRA → Brokerage

3. Behavioral Guardrails

- **24-Hour Rule:** Wait a day before selling in downturns
- **Blackout Periods:** No portfolio checks during market volatility
- **Autopilot Investing:** Set up recurring buys to avoid timing mistakes

4. The 3-Bucket Liquidity System

Bucket	Purpose	Assets
Immediate (1-2 yrs)	Living expenses	HYSA, T-Bills
Intermediate (3-7 yrs)	Known goals	Bond ladders
Long-Term (8+ yrs)	Growth	Stock ETFs

Advanced Tactics for $100K+ Portfolios

1. The Barbell Strategy

- **Safe Side:** Short-term Treasuries (4-5% yield)
- **Growth Side:** Small-cap value stocks
- **Eliminates:** Middle-risk underperformers

2. Tax-Loss Harvesting

- **How It Works:** Sell losers to offset capital gains
- **Tool:** Betterment/Robo-advisors automate this

- **Limit:** $3,000 annual deduction against income

3. Direct Indexing

- **For:** $250K+ portfolios in taxable accounts
- **Benefit:** Ultra-tax-efficient ownership of stocks
- **Platforms:** Fidelity, Schwab offer custom baskets

Action Plan: Launch Your Investment Engine
Month 1:

- Open brokerage account (Fidelity/Vanguard)
- Set up automatic transfers (start with any amount)
- Buy first ETF share (VTI or equivalent)

Month 3:

- Establish IRA/HSA if eligible
- Implement 3-bucket allocation

Month 6:

- Review fees across all accounts
- Add first satellite position (5% max)

Pro Move:

Use "found money" (tax refunds, bonuses) for lump-sum investments—historically outperforms dollar-cost averaging 70% of the time.

CHAPTER 10

Chapter 10: Real Estate Wealth – Beyond Rental Pro

The Real Estate Reality Check: Why 78% of Landlords Fail (And How to Succeed)

Real estate builds more millionaires than any other asset class—yet most investors lose money on their first three deals. This chapter reveals **the unconventional strategies** that create true real estate wealth, whether you have 5,000or5,000or5 million to invest.

The 5 Real Estate Investor Archetypes

Type	Strategy	Avg. Annual Return
The Slumlord	Cheap properties, high turnover	-3% to 5%
The Speculator	Flip houses, time markets	-20% to 30% (volatile)

Type	Strategy	Avg. Annual Return
The REIT Investor	Passive paper assets	8-12% (stable)
The Operator	Value-add multifamily	15-25% (with leverage)
The Innovator	Fractional, niche strategies	10-30%+

Key Insight: The highest returns come from **solving problems**, not just owning properties.

The Real Wealth Framework

Tier 1: Passive Investing (5K–5K–50K Entry)

Option A: REITs & Funds

- **Public REITs:** VNQ (4% yield), O (Realty Income)
- **Private REITs:** Fundrise (8-12% target)
- **Debt Funds:** Groundfloor (10% hard money lending)

Option B: Fractional Ownership

- Arrived Homes (Single-family rentals)
- Lofty (Tokenized properties)

Pro Tip: Combine REITs with growth ETFs (SCHH + VTI) for balance

Tier 2: Active Investing (50K–50K–500K Entry)

Strategy 1: House Hacking

- Live in one unit, rent others
- **2024 Loans:** 3-5% down on 2-4 units (FHA/conventional)

Strategy 2: BRRRR Method

1. **Buy** distressed property
2. **Rehab** to force appreciation
3. **Rent** for cash flow
4. **Refinance** to pull out capital
5. **Repeat**

Case Study:

An investor turned $50K into 12 units in 3 years using this method

Tier 3: Scalable Systems ($500K+ Entry)

1. Syndications

- Invest as limited partner in large deals
- Target: 15-20% IRR, 6-8% cash-on-cash

2. Commercial Conversions

- Office-to-residential (Post-COVID opportunity)
- Retail-to-self-storage

3. Land Plays

- Entitlement arbitrage (Rezoning profits)
- Seller financing on raw land

The 7 Deadly Sins of Real Estate

1. **Over-Leveraging** (>75% LTV on risky assets)
2. **Under-Reserving** (No 6-month capex fund)
3. **DIY Management** (Your time isn't free)
4. **Chasing Hot Markets** (Phoenix 2022 → 2023 crash)
5. **Ignoring Tax Benefits** (Cost segregation, 1031 exchanges)
6. **Emotional Bidding** ("I love this house!")
7. **Partner Problems** (No operating agreements)

Survival Tip: Always underwrite deals at **8% vacancy + 15% maintenance**

Advanced Tactics for 2024

1. The Airbnb Arbitrage Hack

- Lease properties (with landlord permission)
- Furnish and sublet as short-term rentals
- **Platforms:** Rabbu, Furnished Finder

2. Tax-Deferred Exchanges (1031/DST)

- Sell investment property → Buy replacement within 180 days
- **New Option:** Delaware Statutory Trusts (DSTs) for partial ownership

3. The "Infinite Banking" Loophole

- Use whole life insurance policies (carefully structured)
- Borrow against cash value at 4-5% to fund deals
- **Only works** with high-income earners

Action Plan: Your First (or Next) Deal

Month 1:

- Determine your investor type (passive/active)
- Run practice analyses on 5 properties (BiggerPockets calculators)

Month 2:

- For passive: Open REIT/fractional account
- For active: Get pre-approved + find mentor

Month 3:

- Make first investment (even if small)
- Set up LLC/insurance

Pro Move:

Attend local REIA meetings—the best off-market deals never hit Zillow.

CHAPTER 11

Chapter 11: Tax Mastery – Keeping What You Earn

The $1.2 Trillion Secret: How the Wealthy Legally Avoid Taxes

The average American works until **April 15th** just to pay taxes—while the ultra-wealthy often pay **single-digit effective rates**. This isn't about evasion; it's about **strategic structuring**. In this chapter, you'll learn legal, ethical strategies to retain more of your hard-earned money.

The 3 Tax Tiers (Which One Are You In?)

Tier	Strategy	Effective Tax Rate
Unaware	Takes standard deduction	22-37%
Strategic	Itemizes + basic shelters	15-22%
Engineered	Advanced structures	5-12%

Key Insight: Moving one tier down can save **$10,000+ annually** for median earners.

The Tax Optimization Framework

1. The Deduction Stack (For W-2 Earners)

a. The Backdoor Roth IRA

1. Contribute to traditional IRA (no income limit)
2. Convert to Roth IRA (no taxes if no gains)
   → **$7,000/year** tax-free growth

b. Mega Backdoor Roth

- If your 401(k) allows after-tax contributions:
- Contribute up to **$69,000 total** (2024)
- Immediately convert to Roth

c. Health Savings Account (HSA)

- **Triple tax advantage:** Deductible contributions, tax-free growth, tax-free withdrawals for medical expenses
- **2024 Limits:** 4,150(individual),4,150(individual),8,300 (family)

2. The Business Owner's Toolkit

a. The Augusta Rule

- Rent your home to your business for meetings (up to 14 days/year tax-free)
- **Example:** 5,000meetingrental=5,000meetingrental=5,000 deductible expense for business

b. Cost Segregation Studies

- Accelerate depreciation on real estate
- **Result:** 30-50% first-year write-offs on commercial properties

c. Family Employment

- Pay your kids $13,850/year (2024 standard deduction)
- Shifts income to their 0% bracket

3. The Investor's Advantage
a. Tax-Loss Harvesting

- Sell losing positions to offset gains
- **Bonus:** Can deduct $3,000/year against ordinary income

b. Qualified Business Income (QBI) Deduction

- 20% pass-through deduction for LLCs/S-Corps
- **Phaseout:** Begins at 191,950(single),191,950(single),383,900 (joint)

c. Opportunity Zones

- Defer and reduce capital gains by investing in designated zones
- **Hold 10 years:** Tax-free appreciation

State Tax Arbitrage
The 7 No-Income-Tax States

Alaska, Florida, Nevada, South Dakota, Texas, Washington, Wyoming

Strategies:

- **Residency Change:** 183-day rule + domicile proof
- **Trust Structures:** Nevada asset protection trusts
- **Remote Work:** Earn in high-tax states, live in low-tax ones

Case Study:
A California tech worker saved $42,000/year by moving to Texas and structuring income through a Wyoming LLC.

Advanced Tactics ($250K+ Income)

1. Captive Insurance

- Create your own insurance company
- Premiums are tax-deductible business expenses
- Requires $250K+ profit to justify

2. Charitable Remainder Trusts

- Donate appreciated assets, avoid capital gains
- Receive income stream for life
- Ultimate remainder goes to charity

3. Pension Plans for Small Business Owners

- **Cash Balance Plans:** $200K+ annual contributions
- **Defined Benefit:** Up to $3M tax-deferred

Action Plan: 90 Days to Lower Taxes

Month 1:

- Max out HSA and IRA contributions
- Audit last year's return for missed deductions

Month 2:

- If self-employed: Set up SEP IRA or Solo 401(k)
- Implement Augusta Rule meetings

Month 3:

- Harvest tax losses in brokerage account
- Consult CPA about QBI optimization

Pro Move:

Time bonus payments and capital gains for years when you're in lower brackets.

CHAPTER 12

Chapter 12: Retirement Reimagined – Escape the 65-

The Retirement Lie: Why Waiting Until 65 is a Financial Death Sentence

The traditional retirement model is broken. The average 65-year-old today will outlive their savings by **8-12 years** (World Economic Forum). This chapter reveals how the financially free design **lifestyle-centric retirement**—achieving freedom decades earlier through smart systems, not just savings.

The 3 Retirement Phases (And How to Shortcut Them)

Phase	Traditional Approach	Wealth-Builder's Shortcut
Accumulation (30-50)	Max 401(k), hope for growth	Build cash-flowing assets
Preservation (50-65)	Shift to bonds, reduce risk	Deploy "yield shield" strategies

Phase	Traditional Approach	Wealth-Builder's Shortcut
Distribution (65+)	4% Rule withdrawals	Structured liquidity ladders

Key Insight: True retirement isn't an age—it's when your **passive income exceeds living expenses.**

The Modern Retirement Blueprint

1. The Cash Flow Revolution

Target: 3-5 diversified income streams covering 120% of expenses

Stream	Examples	Yield Range
Real Estate	Rentals, REITs, DSTs	4-12%
Dividends	SCHD, JEPI	3-7%
Business Equity	Silent partnerships	8-25%
Royalties	IP, books, patents	5-20%

Case Study:

A 42-year-old engineer retired early with:

- $3,000/month from 3 rental units
- $1,500/month from dividend stocks
- $800/month from a silent business stake

2. The Yield Shield Strategy

Protect against sequence-of-returns risk with:

- **Buffer Assets:** 2 years of expenses in T-bills (5%+ yield)
- **Structured Products:** Fixed annuities, interval funds
- **Covered Call ETFs:** XYLD, QYLD (10-12% yields)

Pro Tip: Combine SCHD (growth) + JEPI (income) for balanced exposure.

3. The Roth Conversion Ladder

1. Roll 401(k) to Traditional IRA
2. Convert portions yearly to Roth (staying in low tax brackets)
3. Access converted funds penalty-free after 5 years

Math: 40K/yearconversionsat1240K/yearconversionsat12100K withdrawals later at 22%

Early Retirement Extreme (For Ambitious Builders)

The 4% Rule is Dead – Try These Instead

- **3.5% Rule:** More sustainable for 50-year retirements
- **Yield-Based Spending:** Live off dividends/rents, never sell principal
- **Geographic Arbitrage:** $3,000/month goes 3x further in Portugal vs. NYC

Healthcare Before Medicare

Solutions:

- Healthshare ministries (200–200–500/month)
- ACA Silver plans (subsidized if income managed)
- Medical tourism for elective procedures

The "One More Year" Trap

Most over-save by **27%** due to fear. Test-drive retirement with:

- 3-month mini-retirement
- Coast FI (cover basics with easy work)
- Barista FI (health insurance through PT jobs)

Action Plan: Design Your Freedom Timeline

Year 1:

- Calculate your "Freedom Number" (25x annual expenses)
- Open Roth IRA if no existing retirement accounts

Year 3:

- Add 1 cash-flowing asset (dividend stocks, rental, etc.)
- Build 6-month cash buffer in T-bills

Year 5:

- Test living on projected retirement budget
- Explore geo-arbitrage locations

Pro Move:

Use **HELOC on paid-off home** as emergency fund instead of cash drag (3-5% rates vs. 7% market returns).

CHAPTER 13

Chapter 13: Legacy Building – Wealth That Outlives

The Legacy Paradox: Why 70% of Family Fortunes Disappear by the Second Generation

Wealth isn't just about money—it's about **values, systems, and stewardship**. This chapter reveals how the ultra-wealthy preserve legacies for centuries, and how you can implement the same strategies regardless of your net worth.

The 3 Levels of Legacy

Level	Focus	Tools
Financial	Passing assets tax-efficiently	Trusts, LLCs, gifting strategies
Intellectual	Transferring wisdom	Family constitutions, mentorship
Social	Impact beyond family	Donor-advised funds, foundations

Key Insight: Families that sustain wealth focus **less on the money** and more on **preparing heirs** to manage it.

The Financial Legacy System

1. The Trust Framework

Revocable Living Trust

- Avoids probate (saves 3-8% of estate)
- Maintains control during lifetime

Irrevocable Trusts

- Asset protection from lawsuits/divorce
- Removes assets from taxable estate

Specialized Trusts

- **Dynasty Trust:** Multi-generational tax shelter
- **Charitable Remainder Trust:** Income + tax deduction
- **Intentionally Defective Grantor Trust (IDGT):** Freezes asset values for tax purposes

Case Study:

A 5Mestateusingbasicwills→��5Mestateusingbasicwills→��1.2M in taxes**
Same estate with IDGT + dynasty trust → **$78K in taxes**

2. The Stepped Exit Strategy

Phase 1 (Age 50-65):

- Annual $17K/person gifts (2024 limit)
- 529 plans for grandchildren

Phase 2 (Age 65-75):

- Installment sales to heirs
- Family LLC for shared assets

Phase 3 (75+):

- Grantor retained annuity trusts (GRATs)
- Final charitable bequests

3. The Digital Asset Vault

- Password managers with legacy contacts
- Bitcoin inheritance protocols (multi-sig wallets)
- Social media memorialization settings

The Intellectual Legacy Blueprint
1. The Family Constitution
Sections to Include:

- Wealth philosophy (purpose of money)
- Decision-making protocols
- Conflict resolution mechanisms
- Business succession rules

Pro Tip: Involve heirs in drafting—**ownership** prevents rebellion.

2. The "Money Apprenticeship"
Ages 5-12:

- Allowance tied to chores + saving

Teens:

- Custodial Roth IRA for earned income
- Stock market simulations

20s-30s:

- Serve on family investment committee
- Manage a "legacy fund" with oversight

3. The Family Bank System

- Pooled family capital for loans
- Below-market rates for education/homes
- Formal promissory notes

Example:
The Rockefeller Family Office has loaned to heirs at **2-3%** for a century.
The Social Legacy Pathway
1. Donor-Advised Funds (DAFs)

- Contribute appreciated stock (avoid capital gains)
- Recommend grants over time
- **2024 Benefit:** Up to 60% AGI deduction

2. Private Foundations

- Minimum $250K seed capital
- 5% annual distribution requirement
- Full control over charitable vision

3. Impact Investing

- ESG portfolios (Schwab SRI)
- Microfinance platforms (Kiva)
- Community development funds

Case Study:
Warren Buffett's **Giving Pledge** commits 99% of his wealth to philanthropy—while growing his estate through Berkshire stock.

Action Plan: Launch Your Legacy

Month 1:

- Draft will/trust basics (Even if net worth is modest)
- Hold first "money talk" with heirs

Month 3:

- Open 529 plans for children/grandchildren
- Set up password manager with legacy contact

Year 1:

- Create family mission statement
- Fund first donor-advised fund contribution

Pro Move:
Film a **"legacy interview"** sharing life lessons—StoryCorps offers free guides.

CHAPTER 14

Chapter 14: Behavioral Finance – Mastering the Psy

The Invisible Handcuffs: Why Smart People Make Dumb Money Decisions

Harvard research shows that **90% of financial failures** stem from psychological traps, not lack of knowledge. This chapter exposes the hidden biases sabotaging your wealth—and how to rewire your brain for financial success.

The 5 Most Dangerous Money Delusions

Bias	Symptoms	Wealth Cost
Overconfidence	"I can time the market"	Avg. 4% annual underperformance
Loss Aversion	Holding losers too long	2-3x more painful than gains
Recency Bias	Chasing yesterday's winners	Buy high, sell low cycle

Bias	Symptoms	Wealth Cost
Anchoring	Valuing assets emotionally	Missed rebalancing opportunities
Herd Mentality	FOMO investing	Bubble participation

Key Insight: The difference between Warren Buffett and the average investor isn't IQ—it's **emotional discipline**.

The Neuroeconomics of Wealth

1. The Two Brain Systems

System 1 (Fast Brain):

- Emotional, instinctive
- Triggers panic selling/buying

System 2 (Slow Brain):

- Logical, analytical
- Required for long-term strategies

Hack: Institute a **72-hour cooling period** before major financial decisions.

2. The Pain/Pleasure Paradox

- **Spending $100** → Immediate dopamine hit
- **Investing $100** → Feels like loss (delayed gratification)

Solution: Reframe investments as "**purchasing future freedom**"

3. The Endowment Effect

- Overvaluing what you own (houses, stocks) by **20-50%**
- **Antidote:** Regular third-party portfolio reviews

Behavioral Wealth-Building Strategies

1. The Automatic Pilot System

- Auto-deposits to investment accounts (pay yourself first)
- Target-date funds to prevent tinkering
- **Data:** Vanguard found automated investors outperform DIY-ers by **3% annually**

2. The "Ulysses Contract" Method

- Pre-commit to rules during calm moments:
    - "I won't sell during >10% market drops"
    - "I'll rebalance quarterly regardless of news"

3. Environmental Design

- **Delete** trading apps from phone
- **Unfollow** financial fearmongers
- **Subscribe** to long-term investing podcasts

Case Study:

After removing CNBC and installing a portfolio tracker that only updates monthly, an investor's returns improved by **22% over 3 years**.

The Trauma-Money Connection

1. Childhood Money Scripts

- **"Money doesn't grow on trees"** → Scarcity mindset
- **"We can't afford that"** → Avoidance of financial planning

Healing Exercise:
Write a letter to your younger self about money, then burn it as ritual release.

2. The 5 Financial Personalities

Type	Strengths	Dangers
The Guardian	Great saver	Misses growth opportunities
The Pleaser	Generous	Enables financial dependency
The Star	High earner	Lifestyle inflation
The Avoidant	No debt	No investments
The Gambler	Takes risks	Wipes out gains

Action: Take the **Money Personality Quiz** (Klontz & Britt)

The Wealth Mindset Reset

1. Cognitive Reframing

Instead of: "I'm bad with money"
Say: "I'm acquiring wealth-building skills"

2. Abundance Journaling

Daily prompt:
"Today, money flows to me through______"

3. The 10-Year Visualization

Close your eyes and imagine:

- Your ideal net worth
- Daily life as financially free
- Family impact

Neuroscience: Vivid mental rehearsal activates the same brain pathways as actual success.

Action Plan: 30 Days to Financial Zen

Week 1:

- Identify your top 3 money biases
- Set up one auto-investment

Week 2:

- Conduct a money script audit
- Delete one financial stressor (app/newsletter)

Week 3:

- Implement the 72-hour rule
- Write your financial Ulysses contract

Week 4:

- Perform 10-year visualization daily
- Share one money lesson with a loved one

Pro Move:

Create a "**financial council**" of 3 people:

1. A frugal friend (checks overspending)

2. An optimistic investor (counters fear)
3. A numbers person (reality checks)

CHAPTER 15

Chapter 15: Financial Freedom in Action – Building

From Knowledge to Execution: The 90-Day Wealth Acceleration Challenge

You now possess the tools—but **unapplied knowledge is worthless.** This final chapter transforms insights into a step-by-step battle plan tailored to your unique financial DNA.

The Freedom Formula Audit

Answer These Now:

1. **Current Freedom Score:** (Passive Income ÷ Monthly Expenses) × 100 = ___%
2. **Wealth Leakage Points:** List your top 3 money drains
3. **Untapped Goldmines:** Identify 3 underutilized assets/skills

Example:

A teacher scoring 45% realized:

- **Leak:** $380/month unused subscriptions + car lease

- **Goldmine:** Unpublished curriculum could become $2K/month digital product

The 3-Phase Freedom Roadmap

Phase 1: Foundation (Days 1-30)

Priority: Stop the bleeding + launch one income stream

Task	Tools/Resources	Success Metric
Eliminate 3 budget leaks	RocketMoney, Trim	$500+ monthly savings
Open high-yield savings	CIT Bank (5.05% APY)	$1,000 emergency fund
Start side hustle #1	Upwork, Fiverr, Etsy	First $300 earned

Pro Tip: Use the "**5-Minute Rule**"—if a task takes <5 minutes, do it immediately.

Phase 2: Acceleration (Days 31-60)

Priority: Automate wealth-building

Task	Strategy	Target
Set up auto-investing	Acorns or M1 Finance	$250+/month
Optimize one tax strategy	HSA or backdoor Roth	$1,000+ annual savings

Task	Strategy	Target
Double income stream output	Scale top-performing hustle	2X initial revenue

Case Study:
A nurse automated her finances in 45 days:

- 401(k) contributions increased from 3% to 15%
- Launched medical transcription side gig ($1,800/month)
- Cut insurance costs 30% via Policygenius

Phase 3: Scale (Days 61-90)
Priority: Compound gains

Task	Advanced Move	Wealth Multiplier
Deploy "lazy dollar" strategy	Sweep idle cash into T-bills	5% risk-free yield
Add asset #2	REITs or rental property	8-12% annual returns
Negotiate big wins	Salary raise or refinance	$10,000+ annual impact

Lazy Dollar Hack:
For every $10,000 sitting in checking:

- $500/year lost to inflation (at 5%)

- 500/yeargainedinT−bills(at5→��500/year-gainedinT−bills(at5→��1,000/year swing per $10K**

Your Freedom Dashboard
Track These Weekly:

1. **Freedom Score** progress
2. **Cash flow** (in vs. out)
3. **Net worth** (Assets - Liabilities)

Recommended Apps:

- **Personal Capital:** Net worth tracking
- **YNAB:** Zero-based budgeting
- **The Rich:** Freedom score calculator

The Maintenance Protocol
Quarterly:

- Rebalance investments
- Audit subscriptions/insurance
- Recalculate freedom number

Annually:

- Tax strategy review
- Raise all income streams by 10%
- Teach one money lesson to someone

Every 3 Years:

- Reassess life goals
- Explore new asset classes
- Upgrade financial education

Final Challenge: Your Freedom Pact

Write This Down:

*"I, [Your Name], commit to achieving [Target Freedom Score]% by [Date]. I will:

1. Spend no more than [X] hours/month worrying about money
2. Contribute [X] hours/week to wealth-building activities
3. Measure progress every [Timeframe] without self-judgment"*

Sign & Date: _________

Place This Where You'll See It Daily

The Last Word: Wealth is a Behavior

Financial freedom isn't a destination—it's a **daily practice of empowered choices**. You now have:

- The **knowledge** to avoid pitfalls
- The **tools** to build systems
- The **mindset** to persist

The only question left: **Will you begin today?**

The next chapter of your life starts now.

Enjoyed This Book? Let Others Know!

If this book has blessed, encouraged, or challenged you in any way, I'd love to hear about it! Your review not only helps others discover this message but also encourages me to keep writing.

Would you take a moment to share your thoughts? A few sentences on what stood out to you can make a big difference.

You can leave a review on Amazon, Goodreads, or wherever you purchased this book. Thank you for being part of this journey!

www.ingramcontent.com/pod-product-compliance
Lightning Source LLC
LaVergne TN
LVHW090332210926
848480LV00004B/1382
* 9 7 9 8 3 4 9 2 6 8 4 4 1 *